THE ENVIRONMENT DETECTIVE INVESTIGATES

Saving Water

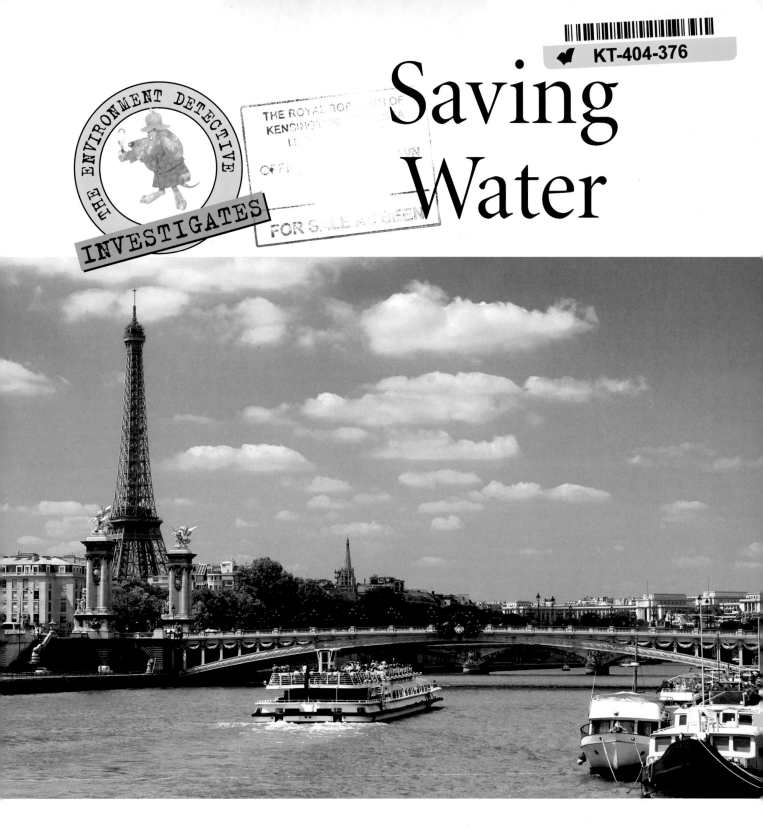

Jen Green

Published in paperback in 2014 by Wayland
Copyright © Wayland 2014

Wayland
Hachette Children's Books
338 Euston Road
London NW1 3BH

Wayland Australia
Level 17/207 Kent Street
Sydney NSW 2000

Editor: Katie Powell
Designer: Stephen Prosser
Maps and artwork: Peter Bull Art Studio
Sherlock Bones artwork: Richard Hook
Consultant: Michael Scott, OBE

British Library Cataloguing in Publication Data
Jen Green
   Saving water. -- (The environment detective
   investigates)
   1. Water conservation--Juvenile literature.
   2. Water resources development
   Environmental aspects--Juvenile literature.
   1. Title II. Series
   333.9'116-dc22

ISBN: 978 0 7502 8096 9

Printed in China

10 9 8 7 6 5 4 3 2 1

Wayland is a division
of Hachette Children's Books,
an Hachette UK Company,
www.hachette.co.uk.

Picture acknowledgements:
The author and publisher would like to thank the following for
allowing their pictures to be reproduced in this publication:
Cover © Mike Goldwater / Alamy, title page © Istock, imprint
page © Istock, 4 © Juan Carlos Munoz / Naturepl.com, 5 ©
Wayland, 6 © Wayland, 7 © Istock, 8 © Istock, 9 © Wayland,
10 © Istock (repeat of title page), 11 © Wayland, 12 © Wayland,
p13 © Mike Goldwater / Alamy (repeat of cover), 14 © Wayland,
p15 © Istock (repeat of contents page), 16 © Istock, 17 © Tony
Waltham / Getty Images, 18 © Wayland, 19 © Getty Images News,
20 © Wayland, 21 © AFP / Getty Images, 22 © Jason Smalley /
Naturepl.com, 23 © Ted Spiegel / Corbis, 24 © Gideon Mendel /
Corbis, 25 © Yann Arthus-Bertrand / Corbis, 26 © Ecoscene,
27 © Tony Lilley / Alamy, 28 © Wayland, 29 (l) © Paul Glendell /
Alamy, 29 (tr) Wayland

Contents

Words that appear in **bold** can be
found in the glossary on page 30.

 The Environment Detective, Sherlock Bones, will help you learn about
water and how to save it. The answers to Sherlock's questions can be
found on page 31.

Why is water precious?

Water is found nearly everywhere on Earth – in seas, oceans, lakes and rivers, in the air and underground. However, 97 per cent of that water is salty. Four-fifths of the remaining fresh water is locked up as ice, leaving only a tiny fraction for living things to use.

Water is very unusual in that it exists in three states in everyday life – as liquid water, solid ice and as a gas called **water vapour**. When water is heated, water vapour rises into the air. This is called **evaporation**. At 0°C fresh water freezes to form solid ice.

Water is made of two common **elements**, **hydrogen** and **oxygen**. A single drop of water is made of millions of tiny **particles** called **molecules**, which are made up of even smaller particles called **atoms**. Every water molecule contains two atoms of hydrogen and one of oxygen, which gives us the chemical formula H_2O.

ECO-FACTS

Ice and sea levels

The amount of water on Earth has remained about the same for millions of years. However, during long, cold periods called **Ice Ages**, more water was frozen. This left less water in the oceans, so sea levels were lower. When the climate warmed, the ice melted and sea levels rose again.

Lagoons by the sea such as this one contain brackish, or partly salty water. Flamingos filter this water to find tiny animals for food.

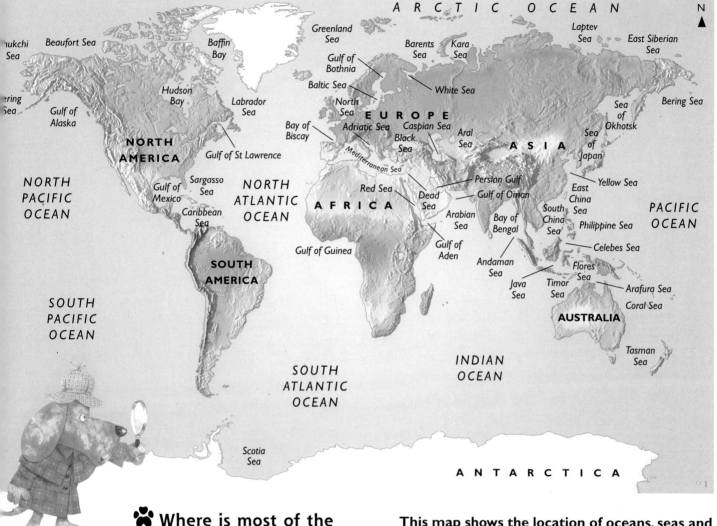

A R C T I C   O C E A N

N ▲

Greenland Sea
Barents Sea
Kara Sea
Laptev Sea
East Siberian Sea
Beaufort Sea
ukchi Sea
Baffin Bay
Gulf of Bothnia
Baltic Sea
White Sea
Bering Sea
ering Sea
Hudson Bay
Labrador Sea
North Sea
E U R O P E
Sea of Okhotsk
Gulf of Alaska
NORTH AMERICA
Bay of Biscay
Adriatic Sea
Caspian Sea
Black Sea
Aral Sea
A S I A
Sea of Japan
Gulf of St Lawrence
Mediterranean Sea
Yellow Sea
NORTH PACIFIC OCEAN
Sargasso Sea
NORTH ATLANTIC OCEAN
Red Sea
Dead Sea
Persian Gulf
Gulf of Oman
East China Sea
PACIFIC OCEAN
Gulf of Mexico
Caribbean Sea
AFRICA
Arabian Sea
Bay of Bengal
South China Sea
Philippine Sea
Gulf of Guinea
Gulf of Aden
Andaman Sea
Celebes Sea
Flores Sea
SOUTH AMERICA
Java Sea
Timor Sea
Arafura Sea
Coral Sea
SOUTH PACIFIC OCEAN
AUSTRALIA
Tasman Sea
SOUTH ATLANTIC OCEAN
INDIAN OCEAN
Scotia Sea
A N T A R C T I C A

❧ Where is most of the world's ice located?

This map shows the location of oceans, seas and ice caps, which hold most of the water on Earth.

Seas and oceans cover more than 70 per cent of Earth's surface. Seawater is salty because it contains dissolved salts and **minerals** that have been carried out to sea by rivers. Ocean water is never still, but is continually stirred by waves, tides and currents. Ocean currents help to spread the Sun's heat around the world. The oceans have a major influence on weather and climate.

Water is important to all living things, including humans. People use water in many different ways, but we don't always take good care of water. Many people waste water, or allow it to be **polluted** by chemicals and **sewage** from cities, factories and farms. We all need to take better care of water, and to use it more carefully. This book will explore how to use water wisely, so our use of water doesn't harm the environment.

DETECTIVE WORK

Use an atlas to investigate where the world's water is located. Which are the largest expanses of ocean? Where are the world's largest lakes? Some of the world's ice is located in glaciers in mountain ranges. Where are the world's greatest ranges?

Where does fresh water come from?

The fresh water we use comes from rivers, lakes, reservoirs and underground water sources. Water does not stay in one place, but is always on the move, and as it moves, it shapes the Earth's surface.

The water on Earth circles constantly between the air, land and oceans, in a process called the **water cycle**. As the Sun heats the surface of seas, lakes and puddles, water evaporates into the air. When warm, moist air rises, it cools, and the water vapour **condenses** – turns to liquid water droplets, which gather to form clouds.

As water droplets collide in clouds, they form bigger droplets. Eventually they fall as rain, especially over mountains and hills. Some rainwater soaks into the soil and is absorbed by plants. The rest drains into streams and rivers which empty into the seas and oceans. And so the water cycle begins again.

DETECTIVE WORK

Investigate how water evaporates by placing a bowl of water in the Sun. How long does the water take to disappear? Investigate how water condenses by cooling an empty bowl in the freezer and then putting it in the sun. Warm, moist air condenses as it touches the cold surface of the bowl.

Can you explain exactly how water changes state as it moves through the water cycle?

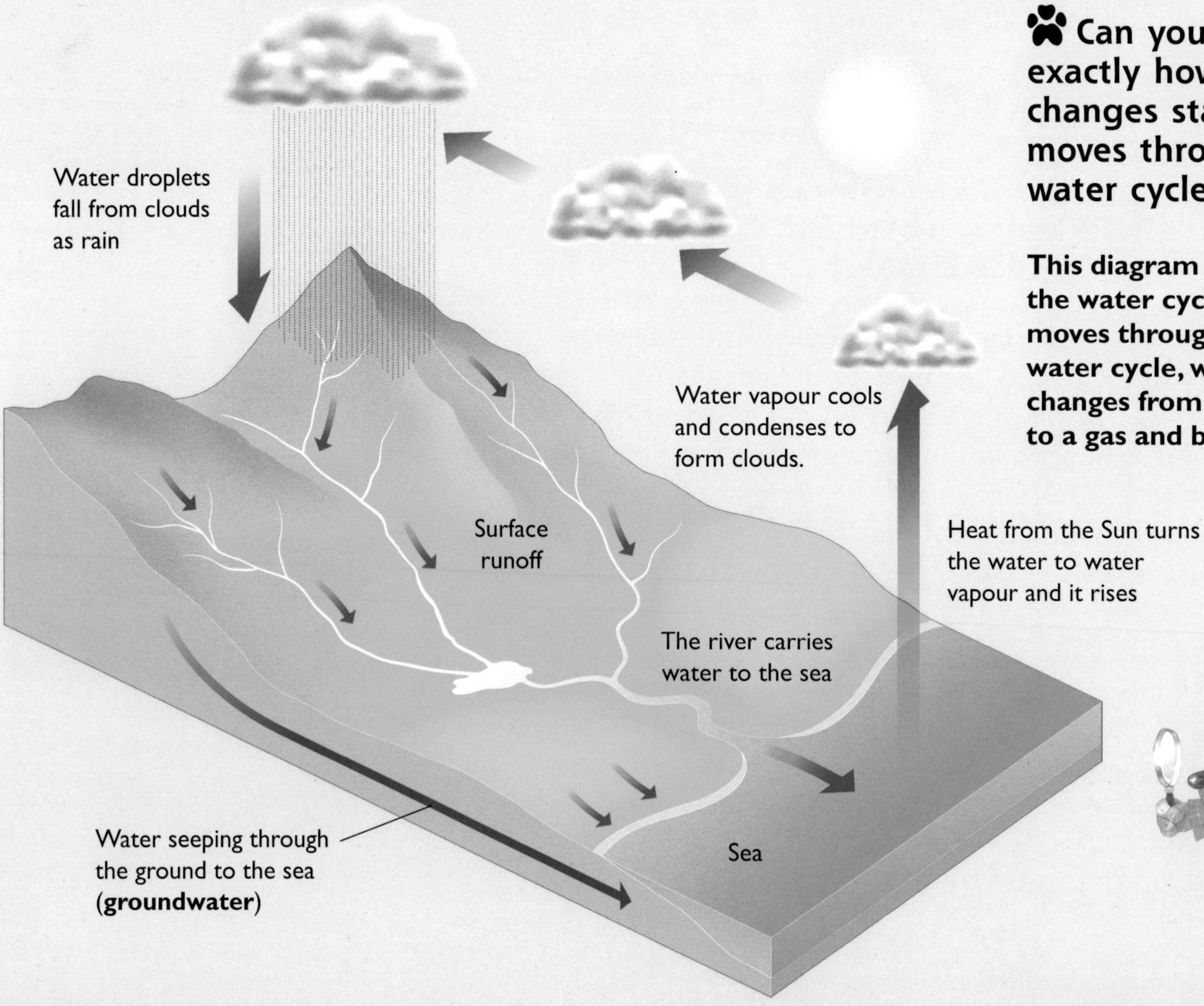

This diagram shows the water cycle. As it moves through the water cycle, water changes from a liquid to a gas and back again.

Water droplets fall from clouds as rain

Water vapour cools and condenses to form clouds.

Heat from the Sun turns the water to water vapour and it rises

Surface runoff

The river carries water to the sea

Water seeping through the ground to the sea (**groundwater**)

Sea

Rivers return rainwater to the sea. As they flow downhill they shape the landscape. Early in the river's course, the fast-flowing water carves away soil and rock to create deep valleys and narrow canyons. Rock and soil are carried downstream and dropped as the river nears the sea, to form **mudflats** or a **delta**.

A fifth of all the fresh water on Earth lies underground. This is called groundwater. After a shower of rain, water trickles down through rocks that contain tiny holes, called **porous** rocks. When the water reaches a layer of **non-porous** rocks through which it cannot pass, it collects in the porous rocks above. The water-filled rocks are called **aquifers**. People dig wells to reach this groundwater and bring it to the surface.

Aquifers are a major source of fresh water for drinking, farming and industry.

ECO-FACTS

The greatest lakes and rivers

Lakes contain more than 50 per cent of all the fresh water that is easily available, and not locked up as ice or underground. Lake Baikal in Russia contains 20 per cent of all available surface fresh water in the world. It is the world's deepest lake, at 1,620 metres deep. Rivers contain just one per cent of available freshwater. The River Amazon, the world's greatest river, holds more water than the next ten biggest rivers combined.

How do living things use water?

Water is essential to all living things, including plants, animals and people. Scientists believe that life began in water around 3.8 billion years ago. All living things also contain a lot of water. Your body is about 65 per cent water – not just in your blood, but in every cell of your body.

Plants cannot survive without water. If a pot plant isn't given water it will droop, though it will soon revive if you give it a drink. Trees and other plants absorb moisture through their roots and draw it up through their trunk or stem. Plants use water and minerals to make their own food and grow. They give out excess water through their leaves, in a process called **transpiration**. Some plants, such as water lilies and seaweed, actually live in fresh water or the oceans. Microscopic plants called **phytoplankton** float near the ocean surface.

DETECTIVE WORK
Investigate transpiration by placing a clear plastic bag over a pot plant. Water the plant first, then tape the bottom of the bag to the pot. The moisture that forms inside the bag has evaporated from the leaves.

Many plants, such as this cactus, use water to stand upright and keep their shape. Water is also used to transport nourishment around the plant.

Water is just as vital for animals as plants. Humans cannot live for more than a week without water. Many animals have similar requirements, although some desert animals get all their moisture from their food. About a fifth of all animal species on Earth live in the oceans, and many more live in fresh water. Most **aquatic** animals have streamlined bodies, which allow them to slip through the water as they thrash their tail, fins or flippers. Mammals, birds and reptiles that swim underwater come up to the surface to breathe air, but fish extract oxygen from water using gills.

Plants and animals living in fresh or saltwater depend on one another for food. Diagrams called food chains show who eats what. Food chains interlink to make a web. Plants form the base of most food chains. In a pond, weed and tiny plants called **algae** are eaten by **herbivores** such as snails, shrimps and tadpoles. These are eaten by **carnivores**. Phytoplankton form the base of the food web in the oceans.

🐾 **Which of the animals shown in the food web are carnivores?**

Water and your body

Every day you lose water as you sweat, breathe and go to the toilet. Sweating helps to cool the body. Your kidneys filter waste and water from the blood to produce urine. You need to drink 6–8 glasses of water a day to replace the water you lose. When your body needs water, you feel thirsty.

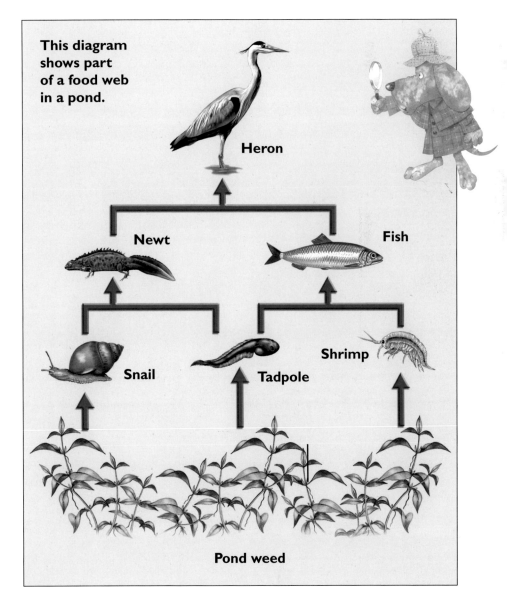

This diagram shows part of a food web in a pond.

Why do we live near water?

In ancient times, many **settlements** grew up on rivers or lakes which provided water for drinking, farming and transport. Today, modern cities still need plentiful supplies of fresh water, so almost all are located on rivers, **estuaries** or near underground water supplies.

Paris, France's capital city, is located by the River Seine. The river is still used to transport passengers and freight.

DETECTIVE WORK

Find the ten largest cities in the world using this website: www.mongabay.com/cities_pop_01.htm.

Which cities are located on rivers or lakes and which are on the coast?

More than 5,000 years ago, the world's first civilisations grew up along rivers in China, India, Egypt and Iraq. People drank and washed in the river. They also channelled water into their fields to grow crops, a practice called **irrigation**. In countries such as Egypt, the river's annual flood would spread rich silt over the fields to nourish crops. Rivers and streams were often dammed to make reservoirs to store water. Rivers, lakes and coastal waters provided useful minerals and food such as fish. Water also offered protection from attack.

Over 4,000 years ago, boats were invented. People used rivers and lakes to travel inland, and later crossed seas and oceans to discover new lands. Ports such as London and New York grew up beside **navigable** rivers or by the sea. Water still provides a cheap and easy form of transport today.

By Roman times, people had learned to **harness** water for energy. Wheels turned by water were used to grind grain to make bread. During the Industrial Revolution in the 1700s and 1800s, people began to use fast-flowing water to drive machinery. Many rivers became centres for manufacturing, and industrial areas also grew up on coasts.

Water use in ancient Rome

The city of Rome was founded in the eighth century BCE at a crossing point on the River Tiber. By 285 CE, Rome had 11 public baths and hundreds of private bath-houses. **Aqueducts** carried water into the city, and sewers carried away waste. The Romans also built aqueducts, sewers and baths throughout their empire.

This map shows the use of water in ancient Rome around 284 CE. Historians believe Roman citizens used five times as much water as we do in the United Kingdom today!

✿ Study the map of ancient Rome. Did the River Tiber supply all the water used in the city?

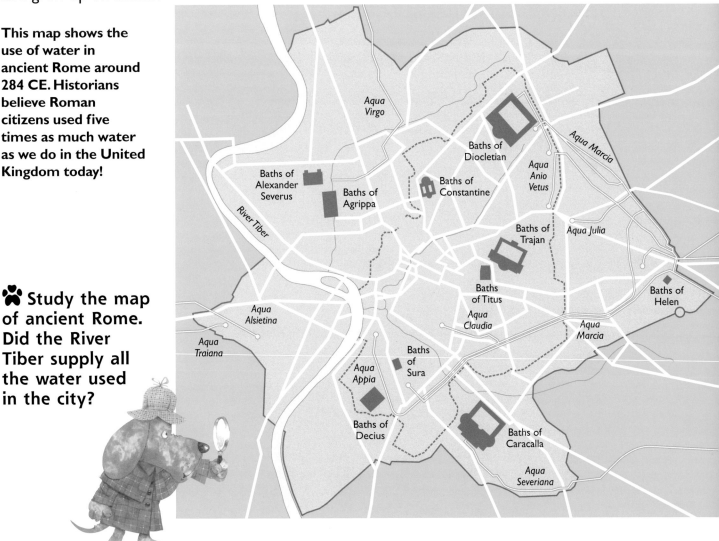

How do we use water for work?

Water is just as important today as it was in past times. We still rely on water for farming, industry, transport and energy. We put water to work in hundreds of different ways.

Growing rice uses huge amounts of water because the crop is grown in flooded fields called paddies.

Experts say about 70 per cent of the world's freshwater is used in farming. Around the world, the total area that is farmed has increased greatly thanks to irrigation. Huge quantities of water are needed to grow cereal crops. For example 1,300 litres of water are used to produce 1 kilogram of wheat, and 3,400 litres for 1 kilogram of rice. Rearing livestock is even more water-intensive. An enormous 15,000 litres of water are needed to produce 1 kilogram of beef.

ECO-FACTS

Hydroelectricity in China

Hydroelectricity is used to provide huge amounts of energy in China. This country has 22,000 large dams over 170 metres high. This is nearly half of the world's total. China's energy needs have increased rapidly as its industries have grown. In 2007, the world's largest dam was completed on the Yangtze River. The Three Gorges Dam supplies energy and water to local cities, factories and farms.

In industry, water is used for washing, cooking and cleaning. In some industrial processes, substances are dissolved in water. Water is also used to transport goods such as timber, minerals and vehicles. Huge quantities of water are needed to make many of the goods we buy in shops, from books and toys to computers. It takes 20 litres of water to produce a single newspaper, and 180 litres to make a bag of cement. It takes 400,000 litres of water to produce a small car – enough to fill a good-sized swimming pool.

Water is also used to generate energy. Fast-flowing streams and rivers are harnessed to produce a type of electricity called hydroelectric power (HEP). A dam is usually built to increase the force of water, which turns giant wheels called **turbines**. HEP is said to provide 'clean' energy because it produces little pollution. Unlike fuels such as coal or gas, it will not run out. However, HEP can damage the environment, because the reservoirs formed by dams change the landscape.

The Itaipú Dam on the Paraná River between Brazil and Paraguay is one of the world's largest hydroelectric plants.

DETECTIVE WORK

Find out how the Three Gorges Dam, the Itaipú Dam and other giant dams are built using the Internet or your local library.

How do we use water at home and at school?

In developed countries, water is usually piped to our homes via the **mains water** supply, so we have water on tap whenever we need it. The use of water in homes is called domestic use.

Litres

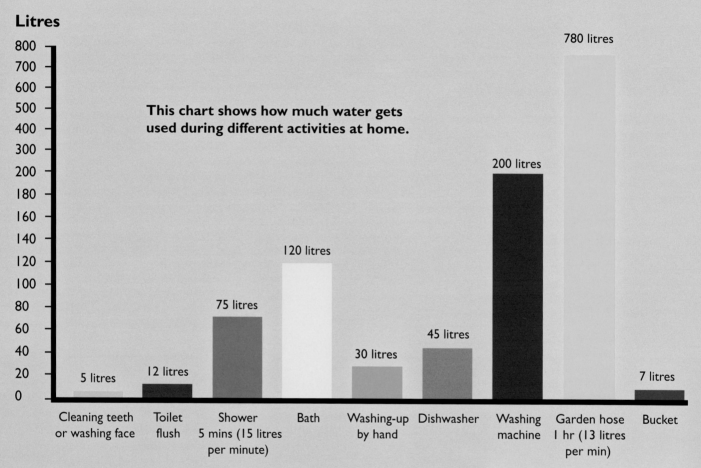

This chart shows how much water gets used during different activities at home.

800
700
600
500
400
300
200
180
160
140
120
100
80
60
40
20
0

| Cleaning teeth or washing face | Toilet flush | Shower 5 mins (15 litres per minute) | Bath | Washing-up by hand | Dishwasher | Washing machine | Garden hose 1 hr (13 litres per min) | Bucket |

5 litres · 12 litres · 75 litres · 120 litres · 30 litres · 45 litres · 200 litres · 780 litres · 7 litres

At home, we use water for drinking, washing, cleaning and cooking. The central heating system that provides warmth contains water. Outdoors, we use water for cleaning cars and bikes, and a lot of water is used on the garden. Indoors, we use water in the kitchen to make drinks, prepare foods such as fruit and vegetables, for cooking and to clean up afterwards. The washing machine gets through a lot of water. In the bathroom, we use water to clean our bodies, brush our teeth, and also for drinking. A lot of water gets used every day just flushing the toilet. The **cistern** (the small tank above the toilet) empties and fills each time you flush. You can save water by putting a plastic bottle filled with water into the cistern. This saves water with every flush.

DETECTIVE WORK
Make a list of all the rooms at home where water is on tap. Include outdoor taps, too. Beside each entry, write all the ways in which water is used, for example, for drinking, washing or cooking.

The number of people on Earth is rising quickly. In 1900, there were 1.6 billion people. By 1950, that number had grown to 2.5 billion. By 2000, there were over 6 billion people, and experts predict the figure will reach over 9 billion by 2050. As the number of people grows, so more and more water is needed for drinking, to grow food and make all the things we need. The total amount of water on Earth remains the same, so pressure on the world's water supplies will increase as the population grows. Experts predict that the demand for water could rise by 40 per cent by 2025.

ECO-FACTS

Water at school

At school, water is used in lessons such as art, science and domestic science. We use water for drinking, going to the toilet and in the changing room after gym or sport. Water is used to prepare lunches. Every pupil and teacher uses about 25 litres of water a day – that's 125 litres every week.

When you exercise you need to drink a lot of water to replace all the moisture you lose by sweating and breathing heavily.

🐾 **Work out how much water your school uses in a week by multiplying 125 litres by the number of pupils and teachers in your school.**

How much water do we need?

Experts say everyone needs at least 50 litres of water a day for drinking, washing and cooking. In some parts of the world, we use a lot more than 50 litres. In other areas people make do with much less.

A huge amount of water is used to water this golf course in a dry part of the United States.

DETECTIVE WORK

Find out about the water supply at home. Contact your local water company, or log onto its website, to find out whether local water is drawn from lakes, rivers or groundwater. Check out your family's water bills. Is the water metered or do you pay an annual fee?

In more developed countries, mains water is available wherever we need it. Many people waste water, for example by using sprinklers in gardens and parks. Agricultural sprinklers also use vast amounts of water. Most of this water soaks into the soil or evaporates before it reaches the crop.

In the United Kingdom and Europe, we use 200 litres of water a day on average – four times more than is necessary. In the United States, people use about 500 litres of water daily. In dry parts of the United States, billions of litres of water are drawn from rivers, lakes and aquifers daily. Experts fear these sources of water could run dry if people aren't more careful. So much water is taken from the Colorado River in western United States, that the river regularly runs dry before it reaches the sea.

ECO-FACTS

Vanishing sea

The Aral Sea in western Asia was once one of the world's largest lakes. It had a thriving fishing industry and was surrounded by fertile farmland. But overuse of water for farming has caused the lake to shrink dramatically since 1960. The fishing industry has collapsed and local farmlands are becoming dry.

This photograph shows an area that was once part of the Aral Sea. The lake is now 50 per cent smaller than it was in 1960.

In less developed countries, there is often no mains water. People draw water from a shared pump or well, or spend hours walking to the nearest river or lake to fetch water. In over half the households in the world, every drop of water has to be carried home in heavy containers. In many of these areas water is also scarce, so people manage with very little water – often just ten or even five litres per person per day.

🐾 **Study the photo of the Aral Sea. What clues suggest the water level has changed?**

What happens when water is scarce?

Water is essential to people and wildlife, but the world's rainfall is not evenly distributed. Some parts of the world have very little water. Other places have the opposite problem – they are regularly hit by floods.

Deserts are places that receive less than 250 millimetres of rain annually. In very dry areas such as the Atacama Desert in Chile, no rain may fall for years. Settlements grow up on the edge of deserts where groundwater rises to the surface at an **oasis**. Elsewhere, regions such as India lie in the path of changeable winds that create seasonal rains called **monsoons**. Many parts of India receive most of their annual rainfall during the monsoon season. Farmers rely on the monsoons to grow crops, but in some years the rainfall is so heavy that it causes floods.

This map shows the world rainfall patterns. Areas that receive less than 250 milimetres of rain are deserts.

ECO-FACTS

Water wars

Where a river flows through more than one country, overuse of water can lead to disputes and even war. In Africa, the River Nile flows through nine countries including Egypt, Ethiopia and the Sudan. Disputes over water almost led to war between these countries until they made a historic agreement to share water in 1999.

🐾 **Study the map. Where are the world's largest deserts?**

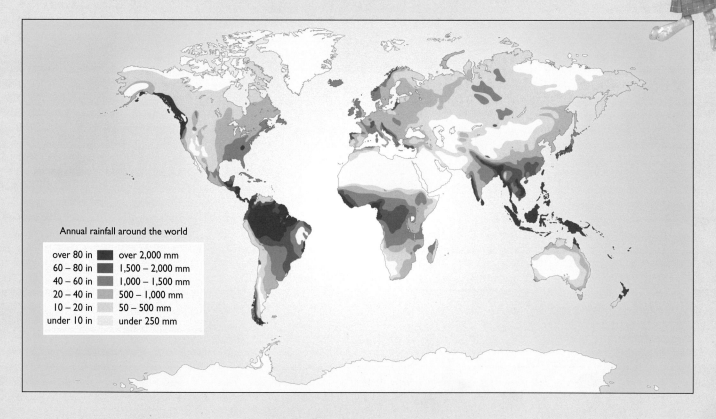

Annual rainfall around the world

over 80 in	over 2,000 mm
60 – 80 in	1,500 – 2,000 mm
40 – 60 in	1,000 – 1,500 mm
20 – 40 in	500 – 1,000 mm
10 – 20 in	50 – 500 mm
under 10 in	under 250 mm

A **drought** is an unusually long period without rain. When drought strikes, rivers and wells run dry. Crops wither and farm animals die of thirst. People may have to leave their homes to seek emergency aid. Two-thirds of Africa is prone to drought, which is also a major threat in Australia, the Middle East and parts of Asia. Forest fires can be sparked by drought. Scientists estimate that 40 per cent of the world's population lives in areas where water is scarce.

Nowadays drought is often in the news, along with floods, forest fires and hurricanes. World weather patterns seem to be becoming more erratic. Many scientists believe that **climate change** is to blame. Scientists are now convinced that climate change is linked to human-made pollution. Waste gases from cars, factories and power plants are collecting in the atmosphere and trapping too much of the Sun's heat. In the twenty-first century, drought may well become more common, and pressure on water supplies will increase.

Ethiopia in East Africa was struck by drought in 1981–85, during the 1990s and in 2008–09. Villagers were forced to leave their homes in search of food and water.

DETECTIVE WORK
Make a rain gauge using the bottom half of a plastic bottle. Tape a ruler to the side. Outdoors, use stones to wedge the gauge so it doesn't blow over. Empty it once a week and add the totals every month. Make a chart showing monthly rainfall.

Why is clean water important?

Clean, fresh water is vital to people's health. In developed countries, people often take clean water for granted, but over a fifth of the world's population has no access to clean water.

In developed countries, water is **purified** before it reaches our homes. At the **water treatment plant**, river water passes through a grid which removes debris. It then flows through settling tanks where small particles sink to the bottom. The water is filtered through sand and gravel, then treated with chemicals that kill the **bacteria** that can cause disease.

The water that leaves our homes is polluted with sewage, detergent and other waste. It has to be cleaned before it can be returned to lakes and rivers. At the sewage works waste water is sieved, then passed through tanks where waste called sludge sinks to the bottom. **Micro-organisms** that digest waste are then added. Finally, water is tested to make sure it is safe. Water treatment is expensive, yet many people waste pure, safe water.

ECO-FACTS

Water and disease

In the early 1800s, many European rivers were badly polluted. Cholera and typhoid were common, but no one had connected these diseases to dirty water. Then, in the 1850s, an English doctor, John Snow, linked an outbreak of cholera to a polluted water pump in Broad Street, Soho, in London. After this discovery, the authorities took steps to improve **sanitation** and water supplies.

Treating water is a complex process. This diagram shows in a simple way how waste water is purified.

1. Water is drawn from the river

2. Water is treated to make it safe. The filter beds at the water works contain tiny organisms that destroy bacteria

3. Water is stored in a water tower until it is needed. Clean water is piped to homes, schools, offices etc.

4. Waste water from homes, offices etc. is cleaned at the sewage works

5. Clean water is fed into the river

In less developed countries, a lot of water is untreated. People have no choice but to drink or wash in dirty water. Polluted water may contain bacteria that cause deadly diseases such as cholera and typhoid. Around the world over two million people die every year from drinking dirty water – and many of them are children. International charities such as WaterAid work to bring clean water to people in less developed countries, for example, by digging wells.

DETECTIVE WORK

Make a simple water filter by putting blotting paper, or coffee filter paper, into the bottom of a flower pot. Half-fill the pot with sand and then top up with gravel. Place the pot into the neck of a large jar. Now pour water mixed with soil into your filter. The filtered water may look clean but it isn't safe to drink.

These women are collecting drinking water that may have been polluted by waste from settlements upstream.

What happens when we don't take care of water?

L ife on land could not exist without fresh water. But people don't always take proper care of water. In some areas, waste from cities, farms and industry is allowed to pollute rivers and wetlands. Plants, animals and people all suffer as a result.

When waste from homes, factories and farms enters a river, it can affect the whole area downstream. Poisonous waste such as chemicals from a factory enters the food chain when it is absorbed by plants and tiny animals at the base of the chain. The poisons pass up the chain when the small living things are eaten by larger creatures, such as fish and herons. In addition, when factories use water for cooling, the water that is returned to the river is often warmer, which can also harm water life.

Algae multiply at the surface of a river that contains sewage or fertiliser from farms.

Chemical spill

Industrial accidents close to rivers can cause serious pollution. In January 2000, poisonous cyanide from a mine leaked into the River Szamos in Romania and the River Tisza in Hungary. The authorities failed to act quickly to clean up the pollution. All wildlife was poisoned for 400 kilometres downstream.

🐾 **Can you explain why the water looks green?**

DETECTIVE WORK

You can test for acidity in rainwater using litmus paper. Fill a glass jar with rainwater and another jar with tap water. Put a strip of litmus paper in each jar. If the rainwater is acidic the strip will turn bright pink. Compare the colours of the two strips.

Many farmers use chemical fertilisers to enrich their fields. But when fertiliser drains off into rivers and streams, it makes the water super-rich in minerals. Bacteria and tiny plants called algae multiply very quickly. The bacteria remove oxygen from the water, which can kill fish and other creatures that breathe underwater. This problem is called **eutrophication**. Sewage which gets into the river can produce the same effect.

Surprisingly, air pollution can also harm lakes and rivers. Waste gases from car exhausts, factories and power stations mix with water vapour in the air to produce a weak acid. The pollution can drift a long way on the wind and then fall as rain. **Acid rain** can damage forests, and when it drains away into rivers and lakes it can kill water life. It can also eat into soft stone.

This lake in Sweden is polluted by acid rain from distant cities and motorways. By adding lime to the water, Swedish authorities are hoping to reduce the impact of acid rain.

What is being done to take care of water?

O veruse of water is stretching supplies to the limit. Water pollution can threaten the health of both wildlife and people. Water is a precious resource which needs to be carefully managed, to look after water supplies for years to come.

Aid organisations such as WaterAid spread the word about the importance of clean water and proper sanitation. They also improve water supplies by installing pumps and wells.

Since the 1980s, environmental groups such as Greenpeace have campaigned for more measures to keep water clean. In many countries, governments and water companies are now working to improve water quality. Most pollution can be removed or treated. For example, lakes that are polluted with acid rain can be treated with lime. But the clean-up work is expensive. It is better and far cheaper to reduce the pollution that enters the water in the first place. Many governments have introduced strict laws to limit pollution. Factories, power plants and water companies that break these rules face heavy fines.

ECO-FACTS

Cleaning up the Rhine

In the early 1900s, the River Rhine was heavily polluted by waste from factories, farms and cities. Salmon had died out in the river by 1940. In 1986, a fire at a chemical factory near the source of the Rhine poisoned the river for 150 kilometres downstream. In the following year, all the countries along the Rhine brought in strict anti-pollution laws. Salmon now swim in the Rhine again.

In the twenty-first century, growing numbers of people will add to the pressure on water sources. Climate change could make the problem worse. Technology can help to ease water shortages. For example, a process called **desalination** removes salt from seawater to produce fresh water. However, desalination is expensive, so most countries cannot afford it. The real answer is to use water much more carefully, and not waste it.

DETECTIVE WORK

Check the health of your local stream or pond by looking for freshwater shrimps and caddisfly larvae. These small creatures only thrive in clean water. Collect a sample of water in a jar. Use a book about pond life to identify water creatures. Carefully tip the water and animals back when you have finished.

Ninety per cent of all the water we draw from taps goes straight down the drain. But clean water is expensive to produce because it has to be treated. In countries such as Japan, water used to wash your hands is reused to flush the toilet, which helps to save clean water.

In a desalination plant seawater is heated. The water evaporates off leaving the salt behind, then condenses to form fresh water.

How can we help to save water?

Everyone can help to protect precious water supplies by using water carefully, and not wasting it. We can also help to limit water pollution. If everyone does a little, it could really help to improve the health of local rivers and lakes.

There are many ways to save water at home. In the bathroom, don't leave the taps running when you wash your hands or clean your teeth. Ask your parents to fix dripping taps and leaks as soon as possible. Taking a quick shower instead of a bath saves a lot of water, too. In the kitchen, rinse soapy dishes in a bowl of water instead of under the tap. When you fill the kettle, only put in the amount of water you need. Ask your family to use the washing machine and dishwasher only when there is a full load. That way, you will do fewer washes. Save the water you use when washing fruit and vegetables, so that you can put it on the garden.

ECO-FACTS

Plants to beat drought

Water is scarce in South Africa. A scheme called Water Wise Gardening helps people to create beautiful gardens with plants that can survive on little or no water. At home, you can save water by asking your parents to buy plants such as yucca and heather, that will tolerate dry conditions.

This woman is watering flowers in a hospital garden in India, using recycled water.

Outdoors, you can save water by using a bucket instead of the hosepipe to wash the car. Ask your parents to install a rain butt to collect water for the garden rather than using the hosepipe.

Oil and paint poured down the drain pollutes rivers and lakes. Ask the council about the best way to deal with these liquid wastes. Strong chemicals such as bleach and detergent can also harm water life. Ask your family to use a little less washing-up liquid and soap powder, and avoid using bleach if you can.

DETECTIVE WORK

Ask your teacher if you can start a water patrol at school. Check for drips, leaks and any taps left running. Your school could install self-closing taps which shut off automatically. Or you could ask for a water butt to water the school grounds. Make a poster explaining why everyone should help to save water.

A dripping tap can waste 25 litres of water a day – more than enough to fill a bath in a week!

Your project

If you've done the detective work and answered Sherlock's questions, you now know a lot about water and how to save it. Investigate further by doing your own project. You could choose from the following ideas.

Practical action

Monitor water use at home. List all the ways your family uses water in one column on a large piece of paper. Ask family members to tick a heading every time they use water over one weekend. Work out the total water used using the chart on page 14. Now beside each heading list ways in which water could be saved. Ask your family to save water and monitor water use over a second weekend. How much water have you saved?

Monitoring water use at home

Activity	Water used	Weekend 1 number of uses	Ideas for saving water	Water used	Weekend 1 number of uses
Cleaning teeth or washing face	5 litres	HHT HHT I	Don't run water	2 litres	HHT HHT I
Toilet flush	12 litres	HHT HHT HHT	Bottle in cistern	10 litres	HHT HHT HHT
Bath	120 litres	III	Have a smaller bath	80 litres	III
Shower 5 mins	75 litres	I	Shower for 4 mins	60 litres	I
Washing-up by hand	30 litres	I	Don't fill bowl as full	10 litres	I
Dishwasher	45 litres	III	Only wash a full load	30 litres	II
Washing machine	200 litres	II	Only wash a full load	100 litres	I
Garden hose 1 hr (13 litres per min)	780 litres	II	Don't leave the hose running when not in use	400 litres	II

Other ideas

- Compare water use in two countries in different regions. One could be in a region where water is plentiful, such as Britain, the other in a place where water is scarce, such as Australia or Egypt. What is being done to save water and tackle pollution?
- Find out all you can about water use on a river such as the Nile or Rhine, or on a large lake such as Lake Victoria in Africa. How is water used by industry, farming and cities? Is water used for energy?
- Find out about the wildlife in a river such as the Amazon, a large lake such as Lake Baikal or a desert such as the Sahara.

Your local library and the Internet can provide all sorts of information. Try the websites listed on page 31. When you have collected the information, you might like to present it using one of the project presentation ideas on this page.

Angling is a popular leisure activity. Fish only thrive in clean, unpolluted rivers and lakes.

🐾 **Sherlock has found out about the mammals of the Sahara desert. Camels can go for many days without water. Animals such as the jerboa (a type of rodent) never need to drink water. They get all the water they need from eating seeds.**

This reed bed is a good place for wildlife, but it is also used to clean waste water. It is a natural sewage treatment plant.

Project presentation

- Write a story or poem about a river or lake from the perspective of an animal living there, such as a river dolphin, otter or heron.
- Imagine you are writing a magazine article or making a television documentary about water use in a particular location. Plan a structure which lists the points you want to talk about in a logical order.
- Write about water use from the point of view of one or two of the following: a farmer, a wildlife expert, an environmental campaigner, a factory owner or a desert nomad.

Glossary

acid rain Rain that is acidic because it is polluted by waste gases from factories, cars and power stations.

algae Tiny plants that grow in water or damp places.

aquatic Living in water (especially animals or plants).

aqueduct A channel built to carry water, often raised on pillars.

aquifer A rock which holds water.

atom A tiny particle in a molecule. Atoms are the smallest particles that exist.

bacteria Microscopic living things found everywhere on Earth. Most bacteria are harmless but some cause disease.

brackish Partly salty water that contains a mix of seawater and fresh water.

carnivore An animal that eats meat.

cistern The small tank above the toilet which empties when you flush.

climate change Any long-term significant change in the weather patterns of an area.

condense When water changes from a gas into a liquid.

delta A fan-shaped area of land that forms as a river drops sand or mud at its mouth.

desalination A method of making fresh water from seawater by removing salt.

drought A long period without rain.

element One of the basic building blocks of matter.

estuary The mouth or lower stretch of a river.

eutrophication Pollution of fresh water which encourages too much plant and bacteria growth, using up the oxygen in the water.

evaporation When water changes from a liquid into a gas.

groundwater Water that flows underground.

harness To use.

herbivore An animal that eats plants.

hydroelectricity Electricity that is made using fast-flowing water.

hydrogen A gas in the atmosphere.

Ice Age A long, cold period in Earth's history, during which ice covered much of the land.

irrigation When farmers water their fields in order to grow crops.

mains water Water supplied to cities and homes through a network of underground pipes.

micro-organism A living thing so small it cannot be seen without a microscope.

mineral A non-living natural substance.

molecule A tiny unit of matter, containing two or more atoms.

monsoon A pattern of winds in hot countries, which bring heavy rain at a certain time of year.

mudflat A low-lying bank at the mouth of the river or sheltered seashore, made of sand or mud.

navigable Of a river that can be sailed by boats.

non-porous Describes a material that is not able to absorb water.

oasis A place where water rises to the surface in a desert.

oxygen A gas that makes up one-fifth of Earth's atmosphere, which animals use to breathe.

particle A tiny piece of matter, such as an atom or a grain of dust.

phytoplankton A tiny organism found in the sea.

pollution Damage to the environment caused by chemicals or natural substances in too much quantity.

porous Describes a material that is able to absorb water.

purify To clean water so that it is safe to drink.

sanitation A system to ensure public hygiene.

settlement A place where people live, such as a village, town or city.

sewage Dirty water from homes, containing chemicals and human waste.

transpiration When water evaporates from a plant through tiny holes in its leaves.

turbine A machine powered by steam, gas or water that is used to generate electricity.

water cycle The constant movement of water around Earth.

water treatment plant A place where water is purified.

water vapour Water in the form of a gas.

Answers

☙ **Page 5:** Most of the world's ice is located in the polar ice caps. Glaciers in mountain regions are also made of ice.

☙ **Page 6:** Water evaporates from lakes, seas and oceans as a gas, water vapour. Later it condenses in the air to form clouds and eventually falls as liquid rain.

☙ **Page 9:** Fish, newts and herons all hunt other animals for food.

☙ **Page 11:** Aqueducts as well as the River Tiber supplied Rome with water. Several aqueducts are shown on the map.

☙ **Page 17:** Fishing boats lie stranded on the beach.

☙ **Page 18:** The world's largest deserts include Sahara Desert in Africa, most of the Middle East, parts of Asia and much of Australia. Surprisingly most land in the polar regions – Greenland, northern Canada and Antarctica – is also desert.

☙ **Page 22:** The water looks green because the whole surface is covered by tiny floating plants (algae).

Further information

Further reading

Protecting Our Planet: Destroying the Oceans by Sarah Levete (Wayland, 2009)

Protecting Our Planet: Threatened Wetlands by Catherine Chambers (Wayland, 2009)

Improving Our Environment: Saving Water by Jen Green (Wayland, 2005)

Websites offering information about water use and conservation

International Rivers network
www.irn.org

WaterAid
www.wateraid.org.uk

Ecoschools
www.eco-schools.org.uk/nine-topics/water.aspx

US government site on water use for schools
http://ga.water.usgs.gov/edu/wateruse2000.html

Conservation organisations

Friends of the Earth
www.foei.org/

Greenpeace
www.greenpeace.org/

World Wide Fund for Nature (WWF)
www.worldwildlife.org/

Environment Protection Authority, Australia
www.environment.gov.au/

The Young People's Trust for the Environment
www.ypte.org.uk/

Environmental Investigation Agency
www.eia-international.org/

Index